# SUNSHINE

## AND

# VICTORY

by

J.C. McPheeters

First Fruits Press
Wilmore, Kentucky
c2012

asburyseminary.edu
800.2ASBURY
204 North Lexington Avenue
Wilmore, Kentucky 40390

First Fruits
THE ACADEMIC OPEN PRESS OF ASBURY SEMINARY

ISBN: 9781621710127

Sunshine and Victory, by J.C. McPheeters.
First Fruits Press, © 2012
Pentecostal Publishing Company, [194-?]

Digital version at
http://place.asburyseminary.edu/firstfruitsheritagematerial/15/

For all other uses, contact:

First Fruits Press
B.L. Fisher Library
Asbury Theological Seminary
204 N. Lexington Ave.
Wilmore, KY 40390
http://place.asburyseminary.edu/firstfruits

McPheeters, J. C. (Julian Claudius), 1889-1983.
    Sunshine and victory / by J.C. McPheeters.
    Wilmore, Ky. : First Fruits Press, c2012.
    64 p. ; 21 cm.
    Reprint. Previously published: Previously published: Louisville, Ky. : Pentecostal Publishing Company, [194-?].
    ISBN: 9781621710127 (pbk.)
1. Tuberculosis – Patients – Biography. 2. Methodist Church – Clergy – Biography. 3. McPheeters, J. C. (Julian Claudius), 1889-1983. I. Title.
    RC312 .M33 2012

Cover design by Haley Hill

asburyseminary.edu
800.2ASBURY
204 North Lexington Avenue
Wilmore, Kentucky 40390

First Fruits
THE ACADEMIC OPEN PRESS OF ASBURY SEMINARY

# SUNSHINE

## AND

# VICTORY

JULIAN C. McPHEETERS

*Pentecostal Publishing Company*
*Louisville, Kentucky*

# CONTENTS

| CHAPTER | | PAGE |
|---|---|---|
| I. | Victor—Not Victim | 8 |
| II. | Three Years In The Ozarks | 16 |
| III. | Turning To The West | 28 |
| IV. | God's Sanatorium | 36 |
| V. | Victors Of The Fray | 40 |
| VI. | More Victors Of The Fray | 47 |
| VII. | The Hallelujahs Of Life | 60 |

# FOREWORD

It is a common proverb, "If the outlook is not good, try the uplook." There is a silver lining to every cloud and a polar star in every night. Life is constantly beset with the fogs of discouragement which would obscure the gleam of the day-star of hope. None of us is exempt from the School of Hard Knocks. Seeming defeat meets us again and again on this earthly highway.

He who learns the golden secret of finding the azure gleam in the night will have learned how to take the remains of defeat and turn it into victory. All of the thorns of life cannot be removed, but they may be handled without defeat.

One of life's sharpest thorns is physical affliction. Discouragement finds fertile soil in a broken body. Despondency is the forerunner of defeat. The path of victory winds the sunlit hills of encouragement.

The chapters in this book deal for the most part with the thorn of physical suffering. The characters described are life-stories which have come under the author's personal observation.

If any who read this little volume find encouragement and a stimulation of faith, its purpose will be fulfilled.

JULIAN C. MCPHEETERS.

# I. VICTOR — NOT VICTIM

I was sentenced to death. I had the death warrant written down in my very being. I was slipping into the grave. I felt the tightening clutches of the invisible enemy gripping my body. A threatening cloud filled my horizon. The ominous shadows which fell across my path were lengthening each day. A short delay in staying the hand of the avenger meant death.

For more than eighteen months I had been fighting a losing battle. I was slipping, and yet hoping against hope. Five different doctors had diagnosed my case with the assurance that there was no cause for serious alarm. Most of them pronounced my trouble as malaria. I willingly surrendered to the time-honored treatment of calomel and quinine, until it seemed to me that I had taken enough to empty the apothecary shops, and to drive all of the malaria out of a Mississippi Valley county.

In the face of all this my condition was rapidly growing worse. A hacking cough, combined with a hectic fever, loss of weight, and night sweats, indicated that there was something seriously wrong. But in the face of it all I toiled on with stubborn odds beating me down. I was at the time carrying a heavy pastorate at Mellow Street Memorial Methodist Church, St. Louis, with a weakened body that was steadily, but surely, growing weaker. Two sermons on Sunday left me quite exhausted. A rising temperature with night sweats followed the fatigue which came from my efforts each Sunday. The battle of each week was to gain sufficient strength to appear in my pulpit the following Sunday. The weeks of such a struggle ran into months, and I was rapidly approaching the point of being forced permanently to bed from exhaustion.

Following one of the hectic Sundays which I was then lashing my body through by force of will, I attended the regular Methodist Ministerial Meeting, which assembled each Monday morning at Centenary Church. While attending the meeting, it was through a ministerial friend, Dr. Ludd M. Spivey, that I learned of Dr. Charles H. Neilson, the noted diagnostician and practitioner. The representations of my ministerial friend convinced me that I should see Dr. Neilson at once.

The office of Dr. Neilson was crowded with patients on the afternoon of February 20, 1918. Many walks of life as well as many diseases were represented by the crowd that had gathered that day in the waiting room of the office in the Humboldt Building in the heart of the city of St. Louis. Many visible signs betrayed the fact that those who were waiting for an interview with the great doctor were battling with disease, and some with death itself.

In that crowd was the writer, an anxious young man, twenty-eight years of age, with pale face and sallow complexion, awaiting a verdict. Ten years of my life had already been spent as a Methodist preacher. I was enjoying a prosperous pastorate, and the future of my ministerial career, except for my ill health, looked bright. God had blessed me with a good wife and two fine children, a girl and a boy, who at the time were one and three years of age, respectively. Although the pulpit which I occupied at the time was quite satisfactory for a young man of my age, rumors were coming to me from the authorities of the Church which indicated the possibility of rapid promotion. But there was one cloud that dimmed the sky; there was one thorn in the flesh—my health.

What would the doctor's verdict be? This was the question uppermost in my mind as I waited in Dr. Neilson's office that day. For months I had entertained a secret fear that I might have tuberculosis; but such a verdict would blight all my future. It would close the inviting opportunities which seemed to be ahead in my church. What would become of my wife and babies? With my salary cut off, how would I be able to live? It seemed that everything hinged on the doctor's decision that day. I was clinging to a faint hope, however, that he would concur in the decision of other doctors, who had pronounced my case to be malaria.

After waiting two hours it came my turn for the interview, and it was with no little anxiety that I walked into the doctor's private office and took my seat. I sat in the presence of a man in the prime of his life. He was head of his department in a great medical school, and on the staff of a number of prom-

inent hospitals. His reputation extended over a number of states. This brought him many patients in
addition to those in his large city practice. I had
a feeling that this man's decision could be relied upon.
The pleasing personality of the man helped somewhat
to relieve my mental tension. He had kindly features,
coal-black hair, piercing black eyes, and a winning
smile with which he greeted all his patients. He was
quick to the point and did not prolong my suspense.
After passing the greetings of the day his piercing
black eyes fell on my face, and with a sober expres-
sion he said: "Mr. McPheeters, there is no doubt
about your case. You have tuberculosis. You have
it in its advanced stages with serious involvement in
both lungs. I don't know whether you can be cured
or not. It depends largely upon your physical resist-
ance and how you apply yourself for a cure. I am
willing to do my best for you and give you every
advantage known to medical science. You must give
up your work at once and go to bed for at least six
months."

Tuberculosis—the dreaded white plague! My
secret fears had been confirmed and my hopes had
been banished. How could I break the news to my
wife and babies? How could I possibly give up my
pastorate and live without a salary? These were ques-
tions I was compelled to meet; I could not possibly
dodge them. I returned to my home that day with a
heavy heart. As my wife met me at the door I broke
to her the news—tuberculosis. She was brave and
sought to encourage me. She said: "We must make

this fight and make it to win." Her words stirred
my fighting spirit, and I decided then and there that
I would do my best.

I notified the official board of my church that I
was having to give up my pastorate, and would not
be able to preach another Sunday. My heart was
broken in having to give up the work I loved and
cherished next to life itself. While many of my par-
ishioners realized that I was in poor health, no one
surmised that I would have to quit so suddenly. My
first Sunday out of the pulpit was an anxious day. I
lived through each service at the appointed hour, and
prayed that I might again be privileged to preach
the gospel.

The first three weeks of my battle were spent in
Barnes Hospital. During this time other doctors confirmed the diagnosis of Dr. Neilson. That I had tuberculosis there could be no doubt. What was the
best course to pursue was the question now confront-
ing me. Should I go West, or endeavor to make the
fight in Missouri? There was one thing that settled
this question for me definitely—the matter of finance.
I did not have the money with which to go West.
It was a question of getting well at home or losing
the fight.

After three weeks in Barnes Hospital I resolved to
return home and place my case entirely in the hands
of Dr. Neilson and do exactly what he told me. The
first thing, of course, was to get out in the open.
Sleeping porches are the exception rather than the
rule in St. Louis. The place where we were living

did not have a porch, which necessitated a move. A move is always accompanied with elements of danger for a tubercular patient. There is danger of over-exertion and of bringing on a relapse. Although cautioned by my doctor, I committed the blunder he warned me against, and suffered a relapse which came near costing me my life. For days I ran a temperature of one hundred and three, day and night, and three cups of moisture per day came from my lungs. Added to this a splitting headache made me at times delirious.

After two weeks I had sufficiently recovered from my relapse to go forward with the treatment out-lined by my doctor. The question is often asked me: "What did you do to make the cure from tuberculo-sis?" The question cannot be answered by naming any one definite thing. There are many elements which enter into the cure of any case of tuberculosis. In the first place, there are no two cases exactly alike. Each case has its own individuality. And herein lies the importance of having a good doctor for counsel and advice. The thing that will help some cases will do a great deal of harm in others. There are, how-ever, certain fundamentals which are essential to all cases. Four of these are: plenty of fresh air, proper rest, proper diet, and proper attitude of mind.

My battle hinged around these four fundamentals. I lived on an open porch for three and one-half years. I never allowed any weather conditions to drive me to the inside. Through winter and summer, rain and snow, I kept up the life in the open. For rest, I was kept in bed almost constantly for eight months. After

I began taking exercises it was necessary for me to spend a large portion of my time in bed. I found by experience that it is necessary for a tuberculosis patient to cut short his anticipated efforts by about one-half. He should stop short of the mark of what he thinks he can do. My diet was measured and directed under the care of a doctor. Milk and eggs comprised a large part of my diet for years. Between each two meals and before going to bed I drank a glass of milk, one-third of which was pure cream. It was fortunate that my stomach was able to care for such a heavy diet. Not all patients can care for so much. For the proper attitude of mind, my religion stood me in good stead. A contented and restful mind is an essential in making the fight, I committed my way unto God with the utmost confidence in his divine providence. I felt that somehow, in a way that I could not see and understand, my affliction would work out for God's glory if I only committed my way to him with a childlike faith.

God was very precious to me in the day of my affliction. I learned anew the meaning of prayer and a simple faith. If my fight should terminate in the death of my physical body, I had faith to believe that I would go to a larger and better land, which would hold for me a richer and a fuller life.

Under the treatment of my doctor as outlined, I soon began to show signs of improvement. Increasing weight each week was accompanied with other favorable signs. These things were encouraging. But my feelings were soon dampened by the statement received from my landlord announcing a fifty per cent increase in my rent. Investigation revealed that the raise in rent was a discrimination against me on account of my having tuberculosis. The object of the raise was to force me to move, and information was given me that an additional raise would be made each month until I were compelled to move. At considerable expense, I had just gone to this place in order to have a sleeping porch, and financially I was already strained to the limit. I had a perplexing situation. One thing was certain: I was facing a move. But where to go was the question. In making another move in the city of St. Louis I might encounter another landlord like the one who was forcing me out. The high price of living would also make it prohibitive for me to continue indefinitely in a large city. These circumstances combined to force me to a quiet retreat in the Ozark hills, where living expenses were low, and where I could fight my battle unmolested by discriminating landlords.

## II. THREE YEARS IN THE OZARKS

Summersville, Missouri, nestles amid the peaceful Ozark hills of Texas County, sixteen miles from the nearest railway station. Here life moves in a quiet, even tenor, without any of the rush and hurry of a large city. It was at Summersville that the thrill of romance came into my life six years previous to the failure of my health.

While holding a revival meeting at Summersville I met a beautiful black-eyed girl, Ethel Chilton, who completely captured my heart. Cupid's arrow had fallen with a sure aim, and the little town of Summersville suddenly became the center of the universe for me. Those were the days before the good roads and the coming of the automobile. The overland trip from the railway station to Summersville had to be made by horse and buggy over very poor roads. But none of these things daunted me. I found myself making repeated pilgrimages to the spot which of all the world had become to me the center of attraction. Muddy roads, deep snows, swollen streams did not keep me away. All these physical impediments were like the fourteen years which Jacob labored for Rachel: "They seemed to him as but a few days." After two years of courtship I married Miss Ethel Chilton.

When seeking for a quiet retreat in which I could fight back to health my mind naturally turned to Summersville. After "chasing the cure" for six months in St. Louis we moved to Summersville. It was a late afternoon in August when we reached our destination. A golden sunset with a thousand colors had turned the western sky into a realm of glory. A dove, in the top of a giant oak, was cooing an evening lullaby to her young. The whistle of a bobwhite calling to his mate broke the silence of the fields. The hush of the evening was upon the air in the interludes of the cooing dove and the whistle of the bobwhite. As the golden twilight kissed away the fading day, my soul revelled in the quietude and peace I had found, as contrasted to the rush and turmoil of the great city. This was the beginning of three years in the Ozarks, a chapter written indelibly in my life.

I was still under the care of Dr. Charles H. Neilson, of St. Louis, whose instructions were carried out through the local physician, Dr. C. R. Terrell. I religiously followed the treatment. Being a good patient is a very important part of making the cure. The local doctor, as he informed me afterward, thought there was no hope for me. The people of the little town prophesied that I would go with the falling of the autumn leaves. But with the coming of autumn, when the first leaves were touched with gold and the green of the field and garden was being seared by the early frosts, I found my condition was turning for the better.

As soon as my temperature approached the point of normal I was instructed by my doctor to begin taking a little exercise. The coming of the cool autumn

days seemed to have a wholesome effect, and I found
that my temperature was approaching the point where
I could begin taking light exercise. In starting on
short walks I was very cautious. I began with about
one block per day; this was increased only a few paces
daily until I had reached two blocks. With slight in-
creases I was soon walking a mile per day. I was encouraged when I was able to walk a mile. This
enabled me to reach a coveted goal, which was the
nearest woods whose leaves were turning to a sea of
gold.

In my first walk to the woods, I sat on a log to rest,
beneath a large, spreading hickory tree. The ground
beneath the tree was strewn with the empty shells of
nuts, whose kernels had been extracted by nimble
squirrels feeding in the upper branches. A gentle
zephyr now and then created a soft rustle, sending
down a shower of leaves to carpet the earth with
brown before the coming of the winter snows. On a
nearby tree a woodpecker was drumming away, preparing his winter house. From a little farther distance into the woods came the contented sound of a
barking squirrel, perched gracefully on a limb near his
winter home, already well laden with ripened nuts.
All the world seemed to be at peace with her Maker
amid such an environment. Being refreshed in both
body and soul, I thanked God and took courage.

The call of the woods made a tremendous appeal
to me, and thither I found my way on my daily walks.
From childhood I had had a profound love for the
great out-of-doors. As a boy, hunting and fishing was

my favorite pastime. My daily walks soon developed sufficient strength to carry a gun. The gun called for a dog, which was soon supplied. With gun and dog, I went forth on my daily walks as happy as a school-boy who had just been visited by Santa Claus. The deep bass voice of a Missouri hound pursuing a warm trail, and later baying at a tree, quickens the blood of the lover of the chase. It was now not uncommon for the bushy tails of two or three squirrels to be dangling at my side as I returned from my exercise.

By the time cold weather came I was walking between three and four miles per day. To add further interest to my walks, I put out a string of rabbit traps, covering a distance of about one mile. Fat rabbits found their way into my traps almost nightly. With these things to lure me, I looked forward eagerly to my walks from day to day. In fact, my interest was so enlisted that I forgot in a large measure that I was sick and fighting a battle for my life.

I continued to follow the routine of treatment with conscientious zeal. I left nothing undone that my doctor advised me to do.

A heavy epidemic of the influenza swept the country that winter, and I was very fortunate in escaping. But another affliction developed toward the close of the winter in the form of a fistula in the groin. This caused no little pain, with much inconvenience. It was a running sore for over two years.

With the coming of the summer in 1919, I had completed almost a year and a half of "chasing the cure." By this time I was able to engage in a little salesmanship to the extent of two or three hours per day. Books and life insurance were the lines in which I engaged. Although I could work but a few hours per day, I met with a degree of success which enabled me partly to check the heavy financial drain of having no income whatever.

A few doctors and many friends advised me never to attempt to preach again. They felt that the speaking would be a strain on the lungs which would cause another breakdown. But I felt that God had called me to preach, and that this was the work he wanted me to do the rest of my life, whether my life were long or short. In the month of September, I returned to St. Louis to see Dr. Neilson for a check-up. The X-ray revealed that the cavity in the upper part of the left lung had walled up. The picture showed it to be about the size of the inner palm of the hand. Two spots in the right lung had healed. There was one remaining spot in the central portion of the left lung which had not healed. The doctor advised that I remain in the Ozarks at Summersville and as yet attempt no move. He did consent that I might attempt a little preaching as a cautious try-out of my strength.

I returned to Summersville and began to do some preaching at the village church. My first attempts were very feeble indeed. I felt that the old-time swing of other days might be gone from me forever. I was forced to speak in a conversational tone, with practically no range of modulation. The old scars and the one unhealed spot on my lung were brakes on my voice. I used extreme caution, however, going in a slow and easy manner, just as when I began taking the daily walks. I attempted to preach only two Sundays each month. After two or three months my speaking began to improve, and was done with much less effort. Although noticing improvement, I was by no means back to normal.

The winter held many danger points for me. I had been fortunate indeed in passing my first winter without suffering any relapse. My second winter was not so fortunate. Not long after the holidays I took a severe case of influenza, which came near proving fatal. Although much weakened and exhausted, after three weeks in bed I took up the battle and determined still to carry on.

The following summer I secured a large tent and pitched it in the center of the town square for a revival meeting. The Rev. W. J. Velvick, my District Superintendent, did the preaching, and Prof. Victor Sears, then Superintendent of Schools at Eminence, Missouri, led the music. Attendance on two services a day, besides other responsibilities in connection with the meetings, furnished somewhat of a test on the measure of cure I had made. During the first days I found myself slipping, with a loss of three pounds in weight. I rallied to the attack by drinking one quart of warm milk, just fresh from the cow, each night before retiring, and by taking more rest during the day. Within a few days I regained my losses and continued through the meetings in fine shape. We had a successful revival, by which the entire community was greatly benefited.

By the close of the summer of 1920 I had been "chasing the cure" for two and one-half years. I had made marked improvement, but still was not ready to cut loose and return to full-time work. In the fall of 1920 I extended my program by preaching every Sunday in the Summersville church. I felt that if I could preach twice every Sunday for one year I would then be justified in attempting to take up the work where I left off when I broke down.

Although my strength had developed to where I was attempting to do more preaching, I still found it necessary to continue the regular routine of treatment which I had been following for the past two and one-half years.

Summersville is a rural community, and I felt keenly the challenge which it offered in religious service. To my mind the religion of Jesus Christ is meant to touch every phase of human life for betterment and uplift. What could I do for the practical betterment of a rural community? Of course my first duty would be to preach the gospel each Sunday, hold revivals of religion, run the church school, youth organization, Women's Society, and other church auxiliaries. But the Church owes something to every community besides the distinctly spiritual ministrations to the souls of the people. Jesus ministered to the physical needs of men in the great miracles which he performed. Physical contacts should lead to the deeper spiritual contacts.

The challenge of the physical needs which came to me in this rural community was that I should do something for the betterment of agriculture. The people lived from the soil. Better farming would mean better homes, better schools, and better churches. I made connection with the School of Agriculture at the University of Missouri, and found the faculty both willing and anxious to co-operate with me in my plans. I enlisted the interest of two county school superintendents (my community was on the line between two counties) and the public school teachers for miles around. This was part of my preliminary preparation for a short school of agriculture, to be held in my church in the early autumn, under the auspices of the School of Agriculture of the University of Missouri. We enlisted the interest of the farmers by mail and through personal invitations. At the opening session of the school our church was packed to its capacity. For three days the crowds and interest remained unabated, and the school closed on a high tide of enthusiasm. So successful was this school that we had urgent demands for another such school in the near future. A similar school was repeated the following spring with results equally as gratifying with those from the one held in the fall.

Mr. A. I. Foard, a member of the faculty of the Extension Department of the University of Missouri, was one of the men who taught in our farmers' school in the spring. Mr. Foard was so impressed with the work that he wrote an article entitled, "Mixing Farming and Religion," which appeared in the March, 1922, issue of *Better Farming*, published in Chicago. As Mr. Foard's article portrays vividly the conditions under which we were laboring at that time, I quote from it somewhat at length:

"This is a true story of a successful country church. Some have said that the country church is going to the dogs. Some churches have gone, and others are on the way. Ministers of high rank have puzzled over the problem. But the right kind of preacher who will put his heart to the task and his shoulder to the wheel can solve it in a rather simple, workable way. Country folks are just as susceptible to religion as they ever were. They hunger for it.

"We stepped off the three-coached train at Mountain View, a small trading center in the Ozarks of southern Missouri. It was eighteen miles from there to our destination, and the distance had to be traveled by wagon, mail hack, or possibly, we thought, by automobile. As soon as the train pulled out I asked the station agent if he had seen J. C. McPheeters in town that day. 'Oh, yes, Parson Mack is here,' he replied. 'He's looking for you. You'll find him at the garage where he's gone to fix a puncture. You've got some rough roads between here and Summersville, but the parson will make it if anyone can.'

"We were soon on our way over this eighteen-mile-stretch of road leading from Mountain View to Summersville. The preacher plunged through mud holes, bounced and bumped over bowlders, and climbed a young mountain near Jacks Fork that set the water to boiling and gave his engine an endurance test. We were lifted up to a plateau country, most of which had been cleared of its original pine and oak, and later of its scrub timber, and was now in farm and grass land. The country was all the way from rolling to hilly, possessed of thin, clay soil, but one that could be improved with proper systems of farming. Decent-looking farmhouses, comfortably but not elaborately constructed, dotted this plateau country, probably on the average of one homestead to every two hundred acres of tillable land.

"We reached Summersville just before sundown. The town consists of two banks, three general stores, one drug store, one garage, one blacksmith shop, two churches, one school building, and about a score of dwelling houses. It is the trading center for farmers for ten or twelve miles around. All commodities must be hauled from the railroad over the eighteen miles of road that I have described, and outgoing products are required to traverse the same route before getting started on the road to the market place.

"My companion, a fellow-teacher from our University, and I had been invited to Summersville to conduct a farmers' institute, or, as it is called in Missouri, a farmers' school. The Rev. J. C. McPheeters, pastor of the Community Church at Summersville, had issued the invitation. McPheeters' church is really a Methodist church, but it is more fittingly called a community church.

"The next morning, promptly at nine o'clock, our school began. It was not lacking in pupils either. The church was crowded; every seat taken. A black board was placed in the pulpit. The local school transferred its classrooms to the little church, the teachers and pupils attending *en masse*. The same was true of four country schools near Summersville. Wagons containing farmers, their sons and daughters, were arriving by eight-thirty. At nine o'clock the church bell called the school to order. Mr. McPheeters opened the school. In way of introduction he said: 'The church is here to serve the community regardless of any religious beliefs or doctrines. Of course the one big job of this church is to save souls, and we are not losing sight of that. But in fulfillment of our great purpose we must render service to mankind. That was what Jesus did when he was on earth. Among the community-building and educational features of the church during the past year we have produced a home-talent play, put on a lecture course, had a Sunday school and missionary institute, held two farmers' short courses, and had an old-fashioned community Christmas tree, where folks put on presents for one another. At our last farmer's school we interested farmers in the matter of improving their live stock, and they are making rapid progress in that direction. We expect to launch into the boys' and girls' club-work as the summer months come. Of course we find some opposition to our course, for there are those who think the church should confine its activities within its own walls. One farmer whom I invited to attend this school said it was "all bunk," and he was opposed to every bit of it. As I have gone out on the streets and roads to invite attendance some farmers have winked and nodded to their neighbors, and joked about young men coming from the university to tell farmers how to farm. But we are making dents here and there. We are progressing, and I am firmly convinced that we are doing the Lord's will.'

"As a definite and direct result of our school about a dozen farmers signed up agreements to co-operate with the College of Agriculture in growing kaffir corn and soy beans, and arrangements were launched for installing a community lime crusher.

"Fate plays a peculiar trick on folks sometimes. Mr. McPheeters was a victim of one of those tricks. He was pastor of a church in St. Louis four years ago, when he broke down with a well-developed case of tuberculosis.

"He filled his pulpit for six months after becoming sick before the doctors were able to diagnose his case. Naturally he received a lot of advice during this time from his friends, most of whom insisted that he go to the Rockies or the plains of the Southwest. McPheeters, believing that there was more in the treatment than in the climate, sought the best doctor he could find in St. Louis and put himself completely in his care. The doctor recommended outdoor life, diet, a blood-building tonic, serum treatment, and complete rest. He then sought the most out-of-the-way place he could find in the Ozarks where he might take this treatment. He moved to Summersville and there fought his battle against that dreaded disease. He followed his doctor's instructions to the letter, and immediately began to improve."

## III. TURNING TO THE WEST

Autumn of 1921 brought to a close our three years in the Ozarks. It was with no little reluctance that we bade farewell to a spot that had been sanctified through a long and painful struggle, yet intermingled with hallowed associations and interspersed with many joyous experiences. And, too, we had learned to love the people of the Ozarks. One of the purest strains of Anglo-Saxon blood to be found on the continent flows in the veins of the inhabitants of the Ozarks. The Indians who inhabited the Ozarks before the coming of the white man were the finest specimens of the Indian race in America. There is something about the land, with its rocks and hills and beautiful streams, that produces a noble race, rich in such qualities of character as hospitality, faith, hope, and love.

Strangely the hand of providence had led us into a three-year retreat in the Ozarks, and strangely the same hand seemed to lead us out. The St. Louis Annual Conference was to meet in Kennett, Missouri, in September, 1921. The approaching Conference was no ordinary occasion for me, for I was planning to take an appointment in a full-time pastorate and resume the work where I had left off three and one-half years previously. The three years in the Ozarks, combined with the regular routine of treatment, had done wonders for me. I had gained thirty pounds in weight and for one year had been able to preach twice each Sunday in the village church. However, certain symptoms still remained which indicated that I would have to use caution. One of these was the morning cough which had not entirely subsided. This cough lasted for four and one-half years before complete relief came. The necessity of regular rest, plenty of sleep, proper diet, and the avoidance of overwork was still very apparent. I knew that caution along these lines was my only hope of success.

I answered the roll call of my Church in September, and reported for work. The Rev. Marvin T. Haw, who was then the District Superintendent of the St. Louis District, had assured me that there would be an opening in St. Louis. As I had broken down in St. Louis, I was rather anxious to return there to take up my work. On the first night of the Conference Bishop H. M. Du Bose preached the opening sermon. Bishop Du Bose was not the presiding bishop of the Conference, but a visiting bishop from the far West. He was looking for two men to fill vacancies in the Northwest Conference.

The morning after I reached the seat of the Conference I was informed by a ministerial friend that Bishop Du Bose was looking for me. Within a short time I was in an interview with the Bishop. He wanted me to go to Missoula, Montana. Such a change was about as remote from my plans as going to the North Pole. I told the Bishop that I did not care to go, as I felt that the winters would be entirely too severe. The Bishop, however, was quite optimistic about the Montana winters, and he pictured in rather glowing terms the virtues of the climate. Only three months of winter and about nine months of pleasant weather was the way the Bishop had figured it out. I was certain that he would not intentionally misrepresent a situation. However, I am now persuaded in my own mind that the Bishop's estimate of Montana winters was based on an exceptional spell of mid-winter mildness which was co-incident with one of his episcopal visits.

After the Bishop's persuasive appeal as to both the wonderful opportunity in the work, and also the virtues of the climate, I gave my consent to go to Missoula. Having received my appointment, I told old friends goodbye, and left the seat of the Conference at once for Summersville, where I was to begin preparation for the long move to my new appointment. On reaching home I found Mrs. McPheeters in much distress about making such a radical change. I found myself using some of the same persuasive eloquence on her which Bishop Du Bose had used in getting my consent to go. Having the true spirit of an itinerant's wife, her mind was soon relieved, and we were both busy in preparation for the long move. I preached my farewell sermon at the village church amid scenes of deep feeling and tender emotion. Our interests had been woven together for three years, in which time we had shared each other's joys and sorrows. I had come into their midst such a sick man that they had prophesied my death by the falling of the autumn leaves. I was leaving in health and strength. I had solemnized the marriage of their living and buried their dead, and they in turn had given me a loyal love and devotion. With moistened eyes and mellow hearts we bade farewell with the heavenly benediction: "God be with you till we meet again."

On the morning of October 17 friends crowded about our little Overland car to bid us a final farewell. The scenes of three years of fellowship together fanned the emotions of our hearts. It was hard to say "Goodbye," but say it we must. In those days it was still considered a long journey to the far Northwest. We were starting late in the season, and were running the risk of finding the mountain passes in the Northwest snowbound.

As we turned our faces to the land of snow-capped peaks where rivers rise, we thought of Abraham who left his native country and went out into a land which he knew not; only we were reminded that it took a much stronger faith for Abraham to make his journey than it took to make ours. Abraham went out into an absolutely strange land, while we knew something of the land to which we were going. He traveled on a camel, while we traveled in an automobile; he slept beneath the stars with his caravan, while we slept in comfortable hotels. As we thought of Abraham we were encouraged, and the difficulties incident to the journey became insignificant.

The Rev. J. A. Baxter, a fellow-minister from the St. Louis Conference, who had been appointed to Butte, Montana, accompanied us on the journey. With

the exception of being snow-bound for one day in
Cheyenne, Wyoming, our delays were of no conse-
quence. We reached Missoula on the first day of
November.

Missoula is a beautiful city of fifteen thousand people, nestling amid snow-capped mountains at the
mouth of the famous Bitter Root Valley, which is one
of the most beautiful valleys in the world. The Missoula River, which enters the city immediately after
flowing through Hell Gate Canyon, divides the city
into two parts. The altitude is three thousand feet.
The city is the converging point of five valleys, which
are all highly productive in agriculture. The chief
of these is the Bitter Root Valley, which is about one
hundred miles in length and is dotted with prosperous
towns along the Bitter Root River. The Bitter Root
River flows into the Missoula only a few miles from
the city. Many smaller streams flow into the Bitter
Root and Missoula Rivers at intervals of a few miles.
These streams have their origin in the melting snows.
They are as clear as crystal and abound in game fish.
It is the fisherman's paradise. The University of
Montana is located at Missoula, which adds much to
its culture and gives it a classical atmosphere.

The environment reminded us constantly that we
had reached a new land. There was something very in-
vigorating in the atmosphere. The snow-capped peaks
which greeted us constantly made us feel that we were
standing on top of the universe. Both the Columbia
and the Missouri Rivers find their headwaters in
Montana.

Someone has said that the people in the West have just two kinds of weather: perfect weather and unusual weather. When we landed in Missoula on the first day of November we found perfect weather. It was very little colder than the country we had left in the Ozarks. But the perfect weather lasted only two weeks. One morning we awoke to find two feet of snow on the ground and a full-grown blizzard in full swing. The wind was roaring down out of Hell Gate Canyon with terrific velocity, shooting the mercury down far below the zero point. It was our first experience in a genuine blizzard. It is true that we had seen spells of weather in the Ozarks which were called blizzards, but they were only "blizzardettes." While the blizzard was at its peak I was assured by my groceryman and other loyal boosters that the weather was "unusual," which statement I did not question for a moment so far as my personal experience was concerned.

The "unusual" blizzard in the middle of November proved to be the beginning of an unusual winter. According to the United States Weather Bureau, it was the coldest winter Montana had had in thirty-two years. Although a tenderfoot, I weathered the periodic blizzards, and came through the winter in good shape. During the winter the last vestige of my morning cough left me. This cough had annoyed me for four and one-half years, and it was a great relief to be entirely rid of it. I also gained a few pounds in weight.

When the robins returned from the Southland in

1922 we knew that the backbone of the long, hard winter had been broken. The summer in Missoula was as delightful as the winter had been severe. The long days of perpetual sunshine turned the valleys into a verdure as rich as that of the Garden of Eden. Thousands of acres of orchards in full bloom sent out a sweet aroma which pervaded the whole atmosphere. Song birds, perched in the tops of the trees and in flower gardens, poured forth golden music. The rippling streams which rushed laughingly through the canyons had abundant schools of the finny tribe, sporting in the sunshine, waiting for the fisherman's fly. All nature was out on dress parade, calling for men to come and drink freely from her fountains of life. It was truly a land flowing with milk and honey. Cool nights in midsummer brought refreshing sleep and rest. By the end of the summer we were fully persuaded that our lot had been cast in a goodly land, and we had forgiven the weather man for all of the severe cold of the previous winter.

During our second winter in Montana Mrs. McPheeters was stricken with a severe case of pneumonia. Pneumonia is very often fatal in the high altitudes. This was also the fourth attack of pneumonia which Mrs. McPheeters had had. Little hope for her life was held out by the doctors and nurses. When the crisis came, it was a battle with death itself. I did much praying in those anxious days, and wired to my friends in several states to join me in prayer. From the human side Dr. Charles Thornton was the physician. He did everything that medical science could do, but he

came to the end of his strength, and frankly expressed his belief in the importance of prayer as our only
hope of turning the tide.

We greatly rejoiced when the pneumonia crisis
was passed. But our joy was soon to be turned to
grave apprehension. Shortly after passing this crisis
a serious complication set in. It was Vincent's angina,
which is commonly called "trench mouth." There
had been two other cases in Missoula that winter,
and both had proved fatal. For weeks the doctors
could hold little hope for us. They were weeks of very
earnest prayer on our part. It was twelve weeks before the fever subsided. That my wife had been
snatched from the grave in answer to prayer, I had
little doubt.

After the long, hard siege through which Mrs. Mc-
Pheeters had gone, the doctor advised that we had
better seek a milder climate. We had become attached
to the Northwest and regretted the verdict from the
doctor that we must go. But we accepted the doctor's
decision as the voice of Providence. This time we
turned our steps toward the Southwest, the land of
sunshine.

## IV. GOD'S SANATORIUM

It was to Arizona, the land of sunshine, that we turned on leaving the Northwest. A twenty-five-hundred-mile automobile journey, leading across half a dozen Western states, brought us to Tucson, Arizona —"The Sunshine City," the great health mecca of the Southwest. The physical environment was designed by divine Providence. Four ranges of majestic mountains from the four cardinal points of the compass protect the city. The Catalina Range is on the north, the Tucson Range is on the west, the Santa Ritas are on the south, and the Rincons are to the east. These ranges stand as sentinels, protecting the city from storms and from the blasts of winter. Living streams are born amid their summits and furnish abundant water for the city and surrounding valley. These streams sink in the sands on reaching the valley, forming a vast reservoir of filtered water only a short distance beneath the surface. This reservoir is readily accessible to powerful pumps, which raise the supply for city and agricultural purposes.

Three hundred days of sunshine during the year justly give the city the title, "The Sunshine City." The remaining sixty-five days are only partly cloudy. Rare indeed is the day when the sun fails to shine for at least a part of the day.

The passing traveler may little dream that the desert at certain seasons becomes a veritable flower garden; but every year it blossoms like a rose. All the cacti blossom, and many varieties blossom in profusion. No finer display of rich colors and refined beauty can be found in all the world than that upon the desert when the cacti are in bloom. The flower of the saguaro, a beautiful, white, waxy blossom, is the state flower of Arizona. In addition to the cacti there are several hundred varieties of flowers which bloom upon the desert. Some of these grow in such abundance that their blossoms present the appearance of a carpet in one rich color covering many acres.

The lure of the desert is lasting when it once grips the soul. Mystic voices are to be heard if you pillow your head on its bosom. If you would hear these voices, go and spend a night upon the desert. Pitch your camp miles away from any spot inhabited by man. A hush and a silence are about you on every side. The sun is dropping toward the mountains which fringe the horizon. The evening is drawing nigh. The hush about you is broken by soft notes from a covey of quail quietly feeding at a short distance, symbols of peace and contentment. A hawk sits upon a giant saguaro in the distance, as motionless as a statue. The mountains lie against the horizon in every direction, and the desert stretches for miles about you. "Put off thy shoes from off thy feet, for the place whereon thou standest is holy ground." You are about to behold that which the artists of the world have been unable to paint. The riches of Croesus and the glories of kings pale into insignificance compared with what your eyes are about to see. The curtain of paradise is about to be lowered before your eyes. Every passing moment brings a change in color upon the sky, from glory to glory. A tinge of purple covers the whole dome of the heavens. Old rose, gold and rich vermilion blend into a divine halo over the western peaks. If your eyes could only pierce the curtain, the angels of God could be seen just on the other side. The twilight brings the hush of the evening upon the desert. The soft notes of the quail have ceased, and the covey is safely perched in a mesquite tree for the night. The sound of no living thing can be heard as the last tints of the twilight fade on the western sky. It is night upon the desert.

When Abraham stood upon the Chaldean desert, steadfastly gazing at the stars, he heard the voice of God calling him to go out into a new land and become the father of a mighty people. When Jacob spent the night at Bethel beneath the stars, he had the vision of a ladder extending from earth to heaven, on which angels were ascending and descending. There is a mellowness in the atmosphere. There is a sweetness in the zephyrs which kiss our cheeks. The stars are out on dress parade, and streams of glory press down upon you from the skies. You are an heir with the patriarchs of old who beheld the glory of God in the heavens above. Sleeping beneath the stars through a peaceful night on the desert is the sweetest rest which can come to the tired body of man.

The curtain that veils the night is lifted gently. The first streaks of the daydawn come tiptoeing over the summits of the eastern mountains. The breath of the morning brushes your cheek, and you are awake. You stand with eyes uplifted toward the eastern hills. The birds are warbling their morning songs. The soft whistle of the quail again greets you. A rabbit here and there is seen dodging through the mesquite and the cacti. A curtain of glory hangs over the eastern mountains as the shades of night are kissed away. The sun in all her magnificent splendor hangs above the last tall peak in the glory of the new day. You have spent a night never to be forgotten. Before you leave the spot you can say with Jacob: "Surely the Lord is in this place; . this is none other but the house of God, and this is the gate of heaven."

## V. VICTORS OF THE FRAY

A customer stood at the window of the Pocahontas State Bank, Pocahontas, Arkansas, making a deposit one day in February, 1925. Charles K. Jones, a young man twenty-six years of age, stood behind the teller's window receiving the deposit. The customer noticed that the young banker had a hacking cough and showed signs of loss of weight, and in passing the compliments of the day made inquiry of Mr. Jones concerning his health. Mr. Jones explained that he had recently had typhoid fever. Following the typhoid he had gone to work too soon, and had incurred an attack of influenza, and the cough was from the effects of influenza. The customer left the bank, accepting the explanation of Mr. Jones at its face value.

Mr. Jones had a promising business career before him. He was married and had a baby daughter. He was treasurer of the Methodist Church in Pocahontas. He stood high in the best social circles of the town. His pleasing personality made for him a multitude of friends. His situation in life reflected the smile of a kind Providence.

It was only the indomitable will power of Mr. Jones which kept him at his post in the bank during the spring of 1925. The hacking cough persisted, and a loss of weight was apparent from week to week. An X-ray examination the latter part of May revealed the fact that he had tuberculosis. The doctor assured him that his case was a very mild one, and a few months in the West would enable him to return in good shape to his regular work. Mr. Jones set his business in order for a Western trip, which he looked upon as a kind of vacation. He expected to return not later than the early fall to resume his work in the bank. Mr. Jones made the trip to Tucson by automobile. Little did he dream that he had imperiled his life in the long, hard drive which he had made. The extra miles traveled, and the days of hard driving which he himself did, were just the things which he should not have done. Experience is a dear teacher, and the price is often fearful.

On reaching Tucson Mr. Jones set about to have an enjoyable vacation, taking but little precaution as to the matter of his health. He did not deem it necessary to consult a doctor. The slight temperature of 99 to 99.8 was not taken as a warning for extra caution. The day of reckoning was sure to come. It is true that some relapses cannot be definitely traced to specific acts of imprudence, but in most cases there is a connection traceable to some such imprudence.

The imprudence of Mr. Jones resulted in a severe hemorrhage. This was a great shock, and his hopes of returning home in the early fall were suddenly blasted. In one sense the hemorrhage was providential, for it caused Mr. Jones to place himself under the care of a physician and begin his fight in an intelligent manner.

Within a few weeks, there were other hemorrhages, accompanied by a temperature running over
one hundred and four. For three months he was unable to feed himself or set foot to the floor. In February he had a natural collapse of the left lung, a
thing which is very painful. In the collapse the lung
is suddenly torn from the pleura, which causes the
extreme pain. After three weeks the lung which had
naturally collapsed began to restore to normal, and
within a month resumed its normal size.

Signs of improvement were again evident, but just
as the tide of hope was rising other hemorrhages came
in June. This relapse meant another summer of absolute quiet. The fall months again brought signs
of improvement, and the tides of hope again began
to rise. But rising hope was again intercepted by
another hemorrhage in the month of October.

On the first of November the doctor began giving
Mr. Jones pneumothorax in order to collapse the
left lung. Up to this time the condition of the right
lung had made a collapse unadvisable. Rapid improvement followed the pneumothorax. By Christmas Day he had gained twenty-five pounds. The
improvement was so marked that it seemed well-nigh
miraculous. Hope was soaring on eagle wings, only
to be pierced by the arrow of disappointment and
brought to earth again. In January Mr. Jones had
the most severe hemorrhage which he had ever had.
For a time it looked as though everything had been
lost. The doctor had assured him that the pneumothorax was his only hope, and now it had seemingly

failed. All the work of eighteen long months seemed to go down in a crash beneath one single blow. The skill of the physician was matched against the seeming odds in the case. An examination revealed that an unexpected collapse had taken place in one of the lobes, which reduced the gas pressure over the cavity in another lobe. The lessening of the gas pressure over the cavity had caused the hemorrhage. The doctor at once increased the gas pressure, which gave the needed relief.

The tides of seeming defeat were turned, and signs of improvement were again apparent. Within one month the doctor started him on light exercise. Within five months he was able to take a full-time position as bookkeeper. Today, Mr. Jones is well and happy and rejoices that he never ran up the white flag while in the thick of the fight.

A thousand dollars per month at age thirty-five is not an income to be despised. C. L. McKee grew up on a farm in Alabama. As a young man his ambition was to become a dentist. He worked his way through college, and, after years of hard struggle, graduated in dentistry. The lean years of getting a start in his profession had passed. At thirty-five his office was located at Twentieth Street and Second Avenue, in the hub of Birmingham's business district. His income was a thousand dollars per month, with a growing practice. After years of struggle in getting a start in the world providence seemed to smile on young McKee. He had been fortunate in his marriage. His young wife and his first child—a daughter, two and one-half years of age—made for him a happy home.

What more could a man ask than to be eminently successful in his chosen profession at thirty-five and have a happy home?  But there was one cloud which hung on the horizon of young McKee's golden day of success.  In 1917 he volunteered for service in World War I, but was rejected on account of his physical condition.  The lure of his growing practice had blinded his eyes to certain ominous physical symptoms which should have been given early attention.  For two years he forged ahead, paying little heed to a persistent cough and loss of weight.

The spring of 1918 found Dr. McKee in the midst of a losing fight.  His weight had dwindled to one hundred and eighteen pounds, and his cough was becoming more stubborn.  For nine months he had driven himself to his office by the lash of will power.  For two years the doctors had been treating him for malaria.  When an X-ray picture revealed spots on his lungs, his doctor advised him to take a few months' rest.  After six months in Florida and Asheville, North Carolina, he returned to his practice.

The improvement which had come during the six months' rest proved to be temporary under the strain of a dental practice.  Six months at the dental chair brought the doctor to the breaking point.  Shortly after dismissing a patient one day in March, 1919, he succumbed with a severe hemorrhage.  After two weeks in bed he went to Asheville, North Carolina, and went into a sanatorium for treatment.  His improvement was rapid, and by the fall of the year he was pronounced sufficiently recovered to return home. Fearing that his improvemment was not sufficient to endure the strain of his dental practice, Dr. McKee moved with his family to a quiet little ranch of twelve acres on the summit of Shades Mountain, a few miles from Birmingham. The quiet and simple life on Shades Mountain furnished favorable conditions for improvement, which continued over a period of two years. At this time his recovery seemed to be sufficient to justify a return to work. For one year Dr. McKee served as the head of the clinic of the Vocational Training School of Dental Mechanics in Birmingham. A vacation trip often proves to be a stumbling block for those recovering from tuberculosis. This was the case with Dr. McKee. While taking a vacation trip another breakdown came, which was followed by severe hemorrhages lasting for several days. The hemorrhages were checked only to recur again within thirty days. The tides seemed to turn for the worse, and for six months there was every indication of a losing fight.

In a last desperate effort to win, the doctor's mind turned to the West. He arrived in Tucson, June 12, 1923, a very sick man. All five lobes of both lungs were involved, and little hope for recovery was entertained by his doctor. For two more years the fight continued, with periodical hemorrhages, followed by periods of relapse. At times it looked as though the long battle extending over five or six years would be lost. One day after a severe hemorrhage the doctor said to his wife: "This will surely be my last hem-

orrhage.  I am going to get well." During the more
than 30 years that have passed (1957) Dr. McKee has
enjoyed long periods of reasonably good health, and
still keeps up the good fight.  He says concerning his
long struggle with tuberculosis: "My sickness has
brought a new meaning of life to me.  It has given
me a vision which I never had before.  You cannot
forget God.  God means more to a sick man than any
other one thing.  My experience has given me a new
estimate of life's values.  I have been made to realize
that the biggest thing in life is not success in a profession or business, but to be able to appropriate the
great spiritual values of life."

## VI. MORE VICTORS OF THE FRAY

Wyatt's book store, in the heart of the business district of Hot Springs, Arkansas, was crowded with customers on the day before Christmas Eve in 1917. A corps of extra clerks were rushing to take care of the last-minute Christmas trade. There was one figure who towered above all others in the crowded store. He was six feet in height, and his weight was about one hundred and seventy-five pounds. His hair, which was beginning to turn a silvery gray, indicated experience and maturity. His features were kindly, and his genial smile and cordial welcome made every customer feel that he wanted to return to the store again.

Mr. L. E. Wyatt, the proprietor, radiated sunshine and good will to all who entered his door. He had been in business for many years and was well known in the city of Hot Springs. He was active in the church and civic circles and was a loyal booster for every good enterprise. His winning personality and good judgment had built up an enviable business. He was peculiarly fortunate in his domestic relations, having a devoted wife and four sons who made him a happy home.

There were no clouds upon the horizon, and the future seemed to hold only increasing good for the years that were ahead. But life is so uncertain! It is possible for the cloud of ill omen to appear on the horizon of earth's most favored at any time. In May, 1918, Mr. Wyatt was greatly surprised one day to have a hemorrhage while at work in his store. While he was surprised, he gave the matter very little serious thought; in fact, he continued to work the remainder of the day. When he went home in the evening he did not even think the matter of sufficient consequence to relate it to his wife. He went with his wife to a celebration in the city that evening and carried their two-year-old son a good part of the distance. It will be no surprise to those who are acquainted with the nature of pulmonary hemorrhages when we relate that Mr. Wyatt had another hemorrhage that night. For two weeks he remained in bed under the treatment of the family doctor. He went back to work, only to have the hemorrhage repeated within a few weeks. The doctor then advised him to go to Colorado and rest for the summer. The Colorado climate did wonders for him, and he returned in the fall believing that he had fully recovered.

On his return from Colorado the doctor advised Mr. Wyatt that he needed plenty of exercise. Being a man who had always done whatever he put his hand to, with a vengeance Mr. Wyatt gave himself to some very vigorous exercise. He was not content with such mild exercise as walking a few miles per day. He had read somewhere in the Scripture, "Whatsoever thy hand findeth to do, do it with thy might." It was the strenuous exercise of grubbing in an orchard that Mr. Wyatt prescribed for himself. Day after day he swung a heavy pick, grubbing roots and sprouts in his zeal to fulfill the doctor's instructions to take plenty of exercise. We wonder that he lasted over a period of months under such a regime, but it was not until Christmas week that another hemorrhage brought an end to his grubbing exercise. After a few weeks in bed with a temperature he was back in his store at work. But he was not to work long, for in the month of May he had another hemorrhage.

The councils of the family were now dealing with a grave situation. After careful thought and deliberation it was decided to sell the business and go West. It seemed to be providential that a buyer was at hand, and the business was turned over in a few days. A large crowd of friends and acquaintances gathered at the train on the day of parting to bid the Wyatt family goodbye. The scene was a touching moment of profound emotions. Breasts heaved with sighs, and faces were stained with tears. Pulling themselves from the fond embraces of loving friends, the family boarded the train bound for El Paso, Texas.

It was on July 4, 1919, that the Wyatt family landed in El Paso. They were in a strange land amid new surroundings. New friends, however, were quickly made, which helped much in making the new adjustment. Mr. Wyatt placed himself under the care of a physician, and began at once to improve. Within only a few months he thought that he was well, and began some work in the real estate business. But another relapse came with a hemorrhage in March of 1920, which temporarily eclipsed the sun in the heyday of high hopes. This relapse was followed with several months in bed. In the autumn marked improvement could be noticed, which continued until the doctors pronounced the case permanently arrested, three years after his arrival in El Paso.

In 1922 Mr. Wyatt purchased a bookstore in Tucson, Arizona. He reached Tucson with his family in August of 1922. Ten years have elapsed as this chapter is written (May, 1932) since Mr. Wyatt experienced any pulmonary trouble. He is well and happy, and is now radiating sunshine and goodwill in his bookstore in the far West. Mr. Wyatt has more than once told the writer of his confidence in a benign providence. He says: "The sifting process which came to me in the years of my struggle with disease has enriched my life. I rejoice in the new friends which I have made in the far West, and I have taken a new lease on life. My confidence in God is stronger than ever." Mr. Wyatt lived for years after moving to Tucson before he went to be forever with the Lord, on August 9, 1935.

On Easter Sunday in 1921, the Southern Methodist Church at Bandon, Oregon, was packed to its capacity. The ladies had decorated the church in keeping with the Easter occasion. For weeks the choir had held extra rehearsals in preparing the Easter music. Every possible preparation had been made to make the occasion one never to be forgotten. The Rev. Clarence B. Holland, the young pastor of the church, had spent many days in the preparation of his Easter sermon. When he entered his pulpit that morning his heart fairly leaped with inspiration in the presence of the large crowd, the beautiful decorations, and the excellent choir. There was just one thorn in the whole inviting setting. It was the condition of the young preacher's throat. For weeks his voice had been failing. He felt keenly the handicap as he faced that Easter audience. As he arose to preach it was with an inward prayer in his heart, "Oh that I only had my normal voice!"

The following month Mr. Holland was compelled to give up his pastorate. His doctor diagnosed his case as tuberculosis. After a few weeks' rest at Milton, Oregon, he returned to his home at Booneville, Arkansas, where he entered the Arkansas State Sanatorium.

Mr. Holland was in his early twenties at the time of his breakdown. He was a veteran of World War I, having seen active service overseas. For six months he had served as Acting Chaplain of the 142nd Field Artillery, 39th Division. He was recommended by his colonel for appointment as chaplain of his company. Only his youthfulness caused the bishop of his church to refuse to make the appointment.

While in the Sanatorium at Booneville the youthful minister met Miss Fay Hawkins, and thereby hangs a tale. It was a case of love at sight. At the end of two months the young minister left the sanatorium and went to Texarkana, where he was united in marriage to Miss Hawkins. From Texarkana they went to San Antonio, Texas, where Mr. Holland entered the Veterans' Hospital in December, 1921. During his first week in the hospital he gained five pounds. Although he was gaining satisfactorily, he was transferred to Prescott, Arizona, at the end of two months.

Mr. Holland and his wife reached Prescott in February, 1922. The long move did not prove beneficial, but seemed to check the rapid improvement which had begun in San Antonio. Prescott has a very fine climate, and one of the government's largest hospitals is located there. But in spite of these advantages, Mr. Holland began losing ground. After a year of discouraging reverses he moved to Wickenburg, Arizona, where he again began to improve rapidly. Within a few months he was able to do some preaching. After eight months in Wickenburg he moved to Tucson in September, 1923. Everything was encouraging until the following December, when he had a severe hemorrhage. For six days he had on an average one hemorrhage every three hours. A bad stomach condition also developed.

After three weeks of absolute quiet Mr. Holland began to recover. He was able to take some light exercise, which was of but short duration. After a month of exercise he developed a fistula, which was a factor contributing to another relapse. This relapse was accompanied by a high fever of 103 to 104, which ran over a long period of weeks in the spring of 1924. The attending physician thought that the end was near. He advised Mrs. Holland to remove him from their home to the Veterans' Hospital as a terminal case. Before heeding the advice of the physician Mrs. Holland decided she would take the case of her husband to God in earnest prayer. One morning she went alone into her room and dropped upon her knees with an open Bible before her. With great burden of soul she pleaded the promises of God in behalf of her husband whom the doctors had pronounced to be dying. At last she pleaded with God to give her a sign if her husband was to recover. She asked of the Lord this sign: "If my husband is to recover, grant that at three o'clock this afternoon his temperature may be normal." She made this request knowing that his temperature had not been under 103 for weeks. She went from her knees with confidence that whatever the sign indicated at three o'clock, it would be authentic. Shortly before three the temperature was still 103. When the temperature was taken at three o'clock, the thermometer registered normal. To make sure of no mistake the thermometer was again placed in the mouth and allowed to remain for five minutes. The register of the thermometer was still normal. Within an hour the temperature was again 103.

Mrs. Holland did not tell her husband at the time of this sign which she believed to be in answer to prayer, but she now had the utmost confidence that her husband would recover. Within a week some improvement was noticeable. While improvement continued, it was a year and a half before Mr. Holland was able to do any work. In October, 1925, he joined the Arizona Annual Conference of the Methodist Episcopal Church, South, and was appointed as assistant pastor of the University Church, Tucson. The writer, at that time pastor of this church, was greatly pleased to have Mr. Holland associated with him.

Mr. Holland's zeal for helping others ran far beyond his strength. On the night of February 10, 1926, between twelve and one o'clock, the telephone in the parsonage of University Church rang. It was a call from Mrs. Holland to the writer to come at once with some ice to help Mr. Holland, who was having a hemorrhage. It was a disappointing message indeed. It meant another year and a half of eighteen hours per day in bed. But after a year and a half, he was again able to begin work. Since his recovery, Mr. Holland has served as the successful pastor of a number of Methodist churches in Arizona and Southern California. He is today (1957) pastor of the Chollas View Methodist Church, San Diego, California.

Dalton Langham was in his early twenties when seized with tuberculosis. He had been converted at the age of thirteen years and united with the Church. As a member of the Church he had served faithfully as President of the Youth Group, Sunday School teacher, and Assistant Sunday School Superintendent. The writer made the acquaintance of Dalton after he moved to Tucson in quest of health. His bed was by a large window where he could see the glow of the golden sunset over the summit of the Tucson mountains. The sunset spoke a mystic message to Dalton's heart.

It was the last week of April in 1929. It had been

less than two months since Dalton had passed his twenty-fifth birthday. An inward premonition seemed to tell him that he would not reach his twenty-sixth birthday. As the sun dropped behind the Tucson mountains that evening a trail of glory was spread upon the western sky. The scene was more like the gateway of heaven than anything earthly. As Dalton looked through the window his spirit was held in rapture at the wonderful scene. As the twilight fell like a curtain from heaven over the earth, Dalton, seen by his mother, was writing a few lines on a scrap of yellow paper. He slipped the sheet among some private papers in the drawer of his table which was at his bedside.

Two weeks later Dalton Langham fell asleep in a faith as quiet and peaceful as the evening glow over the Tucson mountains which had so often reminded him of the gateway to heaven. That day his mother examined the yellow slip of paper on which she had seen her son writing two weeks previously in the glow of the evening. These are the words:

And what if tonight be the sunset of life for me,
   As long as it be a glorious one?
For tomorrow I shall see the eternal dawn,
   In the land of the rising sun.
What does it matter if I have run my race,
   And my work assigned me is done?
As long as I have looked the world in the face,
   I know that I have conquered and won.

"The days of my service are over." This is often the sad lament of the sick person. But this is not necessarily so. There may be a tomorrow in service for even the sick.

Miss Louise Preston, whose native state was Mississippi, volunteered her life for the foreign mission field at the age of nineteen. Before her plans could be consummated she was stricken with tuberculosis. She turned to the West for recovery, moving to Tucson, Arizona. Someone has said: "If you can preach a better sermon, write a better book, or make a better mouse trap than anyone else, the world will make a beaten path to your door, though your home be in a wilderness." Although in a strange land, the beaten path was soon made to the bedside of Miss Louise Preston. As the State Superintendent of the Life Service Department of the Methodist Youth, she became known throughout the state. Hundreds of letters were sent from her bedside every year. The young people loved her, and scores of them turned to her for counsel and advice.

Miss Preston was affectionately called "Louise" by the many who knew her. She was like an angel of light to the despondent and discouraged. She knew the golden secret of prayer, and exercised such simple faith that Heaven's door was repeatedly opened in answer to her petitions. Those of her friends who faced baffling problems often brought them to her sick bed for prayer. Instead of feeling that she must be ministered unto in her affliction, she ministered unto others. The superintendent of the national organization in which she was a state superintendent said that Miss Preston was the most efficient state superintendent in the entire organization. On an invalid bed, she achieved more than those who were well and strong.

The writer stood at the bedside of Miss Preston at "the crossing of the bar." She went as she had lived, with a triumphant faith. She may have accomplished even more during her years of suffering, than if she had gone as a missionary to a foreign field.

It was a broken voice which spoke to the writer over the telephone one morning in July, 1929. "The doctor has just been here, and he says there is no hope for Mr. Clayton. He cannot live many hours." This was the distressing message which came to me from Mrs. Clayton. J. E. Clayton had been a merchant for eight years at Round Mountain, Alabama. On account of failing health he moved to Tucson in December, 1926. After spending two years in bed he had improved sufficiently to be up and exercise and to drive his car on short trips. Mr. Clayton was a lover of the country, and as soon as his doctor released him from his bed he felt the call of the open spaces. He purchased a small ranch, for a home, five miles northeast of Tucson. Surrounded by chickens, a garden, and a small orchard, he lived in peace and contentment in the quietude of the little country home. In this favorable environment he continued to improve, and his family and friends were hopeful for his recovery.

In answer to the telephone call I went to Mr. Clayton's bedside at once. What had happened? An unexpected hemorrhage a few days before had greatly weakened his system, and pneumonia had developed. The end was evidently close at hand. Mr. Clayton had been told the doctor's verdict, and he was facing the issue as calmly as on any morning he had gone to his store in other days. He was forty-one years of age, and was leaving behind a wife and three children, ranging in age from five to fifteen years. In the course of our conversation he said: "I know that I have but a few hours to live, but I am ready to go. My faith in God is my greatest comfort as I come to the end of my journey. I have served him for many years, and now rejoice in his wonderful love. My only regret is in leaving my wife and children to bear the burden of life without my help." After his conversation with me he requested of his wife a pencil and a piece of paper. He wrote a short message to a business friend in Alabama, as follows: "Dear Mr. Griffiths: I have fought a hard fight and kept the faith, but I am losing out. I think it best that it go this way now. Hope you will continue to be able to help Alma as you have always helped me. We all consider you to be the very best friend of the family."

As the day drew to an end a dark storm cloud hung low over the mountains in the east. As the sun was setting fiery lightnings flashed upon the clouds in the east, followed by the deafening roar of heavy thunders. In the east there was a storm; in the west there was the glow of a beautiful sunset. In the physical man the storm of the death throes rocked the body of J. E. Clayton as the storm in the east shook the elements. But his soul rose triumphant above the storm. His last words were those of cheer and comfort. As his noble spirit dropped beyond the hills of time the glow of the evening was upon the horizon. But each evening glow means somewhere a morning light. The spirit of J. E. Clayton slipped away in the evening twilight of the little country home to the eternal morning of that city which "hath foundations whose builder and maker is God."

## VII. THE HALLELUJAHS OF LIFE

*"And again they said Alleluia."* (Rev. 19:3).

Seven years in Tucson, as pastor of University Methodist Church, now bearing the name Catalina Methodist Church, passed swiftly by. During these years, we witnessed many victors in the fray. I saw such triumphs amid the sufferings and the ravages of the white plague as I had never seen before. The radiance of the faces of a multitude, in a losing battle with tuberculosis, still falls as a beacon light across my pathway to stimulate my faith, and to brighten my hope. I repeatedly heard hallelujahs amid discouraging circumstances and saw smiles of confidence and trust on tear-bathed cheeks.

In October 1930, I was appointed pastor of Glide Memorial Methodist Church, San Francisco. There was a marked contrast in my field of labor in the sunshine city, and in the city beside the Golden Gate. The hallelujah triumphs, amid suffering and discouraging circumstances, which I had witnessed during the seven years spent in Tucson, were stamped indelibly in my life. I left Tucson with a sympathy and understanding that I had never known before.

My pastorate in San Francisco, in a downtown church, extended over a period of eighteen years. My next appointment was President of Asbury Theological Seminary, Wilmore, Kentucky. This position

calls for extensive travel over the nation.  Mrs. Mc-
Pheeters traveled with me for some three hundred
thousand miles, by automobile, in this new position.
Mrs. McPheeters was stricken with cancer and underwent surgery, February, 1955.

Shortly before my beloved wife was called to
be forever with the Lord, in January, 1956, we talked over things pertaining to the kingdom of God in
our own personal lives.  We agreed that we had everything to rejoice and be thankful for.  We reviewed
some of the hallelujahs along life's journey.  We
were grateful that we had so many years together.
We talked about some things that we had never talked
about during our earthly pilgrimage.  We expressed
our deep appreciation of how God had come, again
and again, in his divine visitation in our lives.

We discussed a matter that I had never before re-
lated to my wife which pertained to an appendectomy
which she underwent in a hospital in Tucson.  I was
a member of the board of trustees of the hospital
and requested that I might witness the operation.
They granted my request.  They put a white, doctor's
robe on me, and I stood by to witness the operation.
I was concerned lest Mrs. McPheeters' heart might
not hold up, for in those days she had heart trouble.
In the midst of the operation, after the incision had
been made, her heart stopped.  Her face turned black.
The physician and his assistants dropped their instru-
ment and rushed around her immediately, throwing
an oxygen mask over her face.  One doctor manipu-
lated her lungs, while the others administered every-

thing known to medical science to revive the heart that had suddenly stopped. That was the most painful moment of my life up until that time.

But the heart began to beat again, and color came back to her face. Our prayers were answered. I shall never forget the hallelujah that went up from my heart at that time, a hallelujah of praise to God for sparing my companion, and lengthening her years, for the rearing of our children.

We discussed another crucial event which transpired in Missoula, Montana, where Mrs. McPheeters had pneumonia for the fourth time in her life, which event has already been referred to. Vincent's angina, commonly known as trench mouth, developed in connection with the pneumonia. For twelve weeks she had a high fever, lingering between life and death, with as many as three doctors a day in the home, and nurses day and night. At the point when death was seemingly upon her, the nurse said to me: "I am afraid to take my eyes off her, for each breath seems to be the last."

The tide turned. We were praying day and night. I retired for an hour of sleep. When I awoke, the nurse said: "There is a little sign of improvement." She was restored to us. During that painful period, I saw her look into the face of the doctor, and heard her say with the earnest plea of a mother's heart: "Oh, doctor, save me if you can, for the sake of my children." Again we said hallelujah when God raised her up.

When Christ came into my heart as a child, there

was a hallelujah in my heart for such a great salvation.

The day came, when as a Christian, I discovered an inner impediment and a battle within, a struggle that Paul describes in the 7th chapter of Romans: "For the good that I would, I do not: but the evil which I would not, that I do." I found deliverance in the Lord Jesus Christ, a Saviour who is able to cleanse from the inner roots of bitterness and fill the heart with the Holy Spirit. Paul breaks forth in praise saying: "I thank God through Jesus Christ our Lord." Paul was saying, "Hallelujah", for deliverance from all sin as he came to the close of that 7th chapter of Romans.

There is a final hallelujah, as relates to this life. Rev. Joseph H. Smith, the well known Bible expositor, was my teacher for a time in Meridian College. In one of his classes he said: "Young men, there is a difference between dying and death. Dying is the ordeal through which all must pass physically." Dying may entail agony, suffering and conflict. But death is the doorway of triumph to the city of God. Christ speaks of this triumph in these words: "Death is swallowed up in victory. O death, where is thy sting? O grave, where is thy victory?" (I Cor. 15:54, 55).

As my wife approached "the valley of the shadow" I felt the mystic chariot near, commanded by the angels of God. My faith leads me to believe that there was a Hallelujah, when she stepped in the chariot, and the angels in command bore her away to the eternal city. "And I John saw the holy city, new Jerusalem, coming down from God out of heaven, prepared as a bride adorned for her husband. And God shall wipe away all tears from their eyes: and there shall be no more death, neither sorrow, nor crying, neither shall there be any more pain: for the former things are passed away." "And again they said Hallelujah." "When we've been there ten thousand years, we'll have no less days to sing God's praise," and say Hallelujah, "than when we first begun."